## What's in this book

This book belongs to

T0351521

_____

# 生日快乐! Happy birthday!

## 学习内容 Contents

### 沟通 Communication

问事情怎么做
Ask about how to do something

祝贺他人
Express good wishes to someone

背景介绍：
浩浩在回想去年生日时全家人帮他庆祝生日的情景。

### 生词 New words

| | | |
|---|---|---|
| ★ | 今天 | today |
| ★ | 明天 | tomorrow |
| ★ | 昨天 | yesterday |
| ★ | 怎么 | how |
| ★ | 生日 | birthday |
| ★ | 快乐 | happy |
| ★ | 蛋糕 | cake |
| | 祝 | to wish |
| | 做 | to make |
| | 块 | piece |

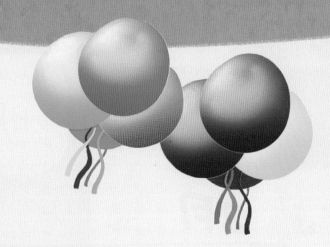

## 句式 Sentence patterns

怎么庆祝呢?
How to celebrate?

祝你生日快乐!
Happy birthday to you!

## 跨学科学习 Project

认识不同国家的地理位置
Learn about the geographic
locations of different countries

## 文化 Cultures

不同国家的传统生日食物
Traditional birthday food
from around the world

参考答案:
1  My birthday is on 27 April/5 October.
2  I celebrate my birthday with my family and friends.
3  Yes, he did.

## Get ready

**1** When is your birthday?

**2** How do you usually celebrate your birthday?

**3** Do you think Hao Hao liked his birthday party last year?

## 读一读 Read

míng tiān
# 明天

"明天"是"今天"的后一天。

故事大意：
浩浩在他生日当天失望地发现家人似乎都忘了他的生日。正当他失落之时，大家拿着蛋糕和礼物走出来，原来家人为他准备了一个惊喜派对。

# 明天是浩浩的生日。

参考问题和答案：

1 What day is it today? (It is 7 February.)

2 What day is it tomorrow? (It is 8 February.)

3 Is tomorrow a special day? (Yes, it is. It is Hao Hao's birthday.)

参考问题和答案：

1  What time is it? (It is one thirty in the morning.)
2  Why is Hao Hao still awake? (Because he is very excited about his birthday.)
3  What is on Hao Hao's mind? (He is thinking about how he is going to celebrate his birthday, and what presents he is going to receive.)

询问情状、性质、方式、原因、行动等的时候，我们可以说"怎么……"。

zěn    me
怎么

怎么庆祝呢？礼物是什么呢？玩具？文具？

**2月**

| 日 | 一 | 二 | 三 | 四 | 五 | 六 |
| --- | --- | --- | --- | --- | --- | --- |
|  |  |  | 1 | 2 | 3 | 4 |
| 5 | 6 | 7 | 8 | 9 | 10 | 11 |
| 12 | 13 | 14 | 15 | 16 | 17 | 18 |
| 19 | 20 | 21 | 22 | 23 | 24 | 25 |
| 26 | 27 | 28 |  |  |  |  |

jīn tiān
今 天

参考问题和答案：

1 What day is it today? (It is 8 February, Hao Hao's birthday.)

2 Why does Hao Hao look unhappy? (Because he cannot find anyone in the house. He thinks nobody remembered his birthday.)

今天是浩浩的生日。
"你们在哪里？"浩浩说。

zhù nǐ shēng rì kuài lè

祝你生日快乐!

在祝贺别人生日时我们可以说"生日快乐!"或"祝你生日快乐!"

"祝你生日快乐!"大家一起说。

参考问题和答案:

1 Did Hao Hao's family forget his birthday? (No, they did not.)
2 What do you think everyone is saying to Hao Hao? ('Happy birthday!')
3 Does Hao Hao look happy? (Yes, he is surprised and very happy.)

zuó tiān
**昨天**

"昨天"是"今天"的前一天。

dàn gāo
**蛋糕**

"这是我和妈妈昨天做的蛋糕。"姐姐说。

参考问题和答案：
What did Hao Hao's family do yesterday? (Ling Ling and Mum made him a cake. Dad made him a model plane.)

延伸活动：
问问学生有没有跟浩浩类似的经历，他们最难忘的生日是怎么样的。

"我们没有忘记你的生日。"妈妈说。

参考问题和答案：
Do you think Hao Hao likes his birthday surprise? (Yes, he does.)

# Let's think

**1** Number the pictures in order. Write in Chinese.

二　三　一　四

**2** Discuss different elements of a story with your friend. Circle your answers.

告诉学生，一个故事要有主题，此外，场景和人物也是故事的基本元素，而一个故事要有趣就必须要有一个矛盾冲突，以形成高潮。本故事的主题是浩浩的生日，冲突是浩浩满心期待自己的生日，却在生日那天失望地发现家人似乎都忘了他的生日。而高潮部分，则是浩浩家人捧着生日蛋糕和礼物，给了他一个惊喜。

**Characters**

**Setting**

**Theme**

**Problem**

**Solution/Result**

# New words

**1** Learn the new words.

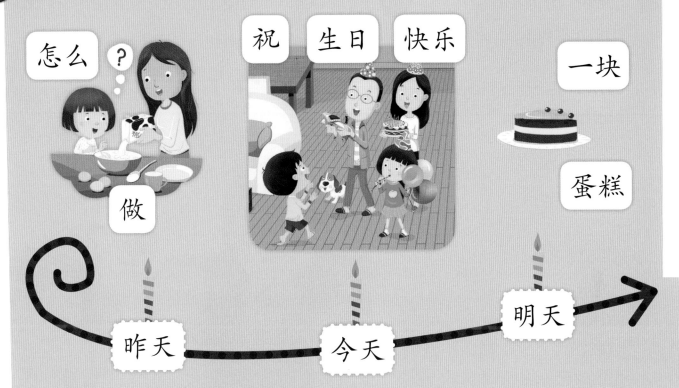

怎么 ?

做

祝　生日　快乐

一块

蛋糕

昨天　　今天　　明天

**2** Look at the pictures. Write the letters.

a 明天　b 昨天　c 今天　d 蛋糕　e 生日快乐

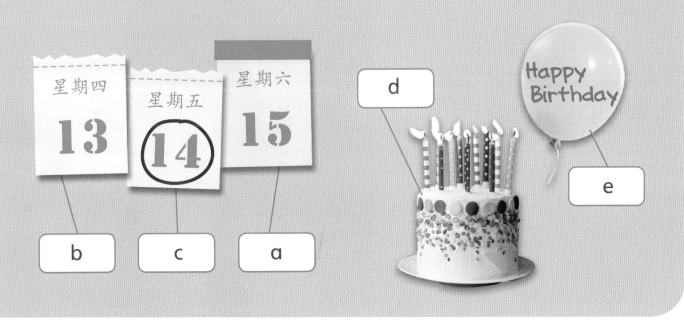

星期四 **13**　星期五 **(14)**　星期六 **15**

b　c　a

d

Happy Birthday

e

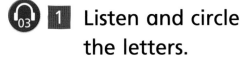
听听说说 Listen and say

第一题录音稿：
1 昨天是爱莎的生日，今天是浩浩的生日。
2 浩浩的生日，爸爸送他飞机，妈妈送蛋糕。
3 男孩：我今天生日，我七岁了。
  女孩：祝你生日快乐！

**1** Listen and circle the letters.

**1** When is Hao Hao's birthday?

a 明天

(b) 今天

c 昨天

**2** What birthday present does Mum give Hao Hao?

a 飞机

(b) 蛋糕

c 块

**3** What does the girl say to the boy?

a 我今天生日。

b 我七岁了。

(c) 祝你生日快乐！

**2** Look at the picture. Listen to the story.

第二题参考问题和答案：

1 When did Mum, Dad and Hao Hao make the birthday cake? Answer in Chinese. (昨天。)

2 What did you do for your parents' birthdays? (I wrote them birthday cards./I made Dad a birthday cake and sent flowers to Mum.)

d say.

# Task

Call your friend and ask him/her about his/her birthday.

昨天是你的生日吗？
你们怎么庆祝？

昨天是我的生日，我和爸爸、妈妈、姐姐、爷爷、奶奶一起唱歌、吃蛋糕。

祝你生日快乐！

# Game

Find out when your friends' birthdays are and congratulate them.

朋友的生日
6 7 8 9 10 11 12

十月是爱莎的生日。

祝你生日快乐！

# Song

🎧 06 **Listen and sing.**

祝你生日快乐，

祝你生日快乐，

祝你生日快乐，

祝你生日快乐。

延伸活动：
问问学生会不会用其他语言唱这首歌，如果会的可以为全班表演。

## 课堂用语 Classroom language

告诉大家。
**Tell everyone.**

告诉朋友。
**Tell your friend.**

问朋友。
**Ask your friend.**

**1** Learn and trace the stroke. 老师示范笔画动作，学生跟着做：用手在空中画出"卧钩"。

卧钩

**2** Learn the component. Colour 心 in the characters red.

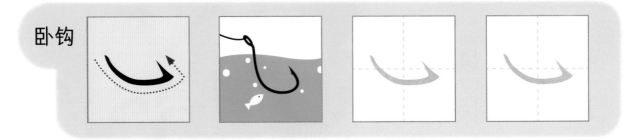

怎 您 忘 想

引导学生发现"心"字与心脏、心情有关。

**3** Chinese people describe many feelings with 心. Can you guess what the words mean?

开心

担心

伤心

学生根据老师的描述猜测和理解生词的意思：打开关闭的心，感觉高兴、快乐；把心抗在肩上，感觉忧虑；一个人的心受伤了，感觉难过、悲伤。

**4** Trace and write the character.

怎 怎 怎

**5** Write and say.  小女孩想知道做蛋糕的方法，问问学生，她应该用哪个词来问妈妈。

妈妈，我们  么做蛋糕？

## 汉字小常识 Did you know?

The shape of a component can change according to its position in the character.

Study the characters. Trace the components.

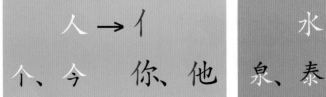

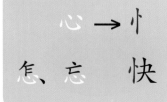

| 人 → 亻 | 水 → 氵 | 心 → 忄 |
|---|---|---|
| 个、今  你、他 | 泉、泰  浩 | 怎、忘  快 |

## Cultures

**People around the world celebrate birthdays. Do you know what food they have on their birthdays?**

中国人生日吃长长的"长寿面"，寓意健康长寿。
红鸡蛋代表喜庆吉祥。

People have different food on their birthdays according to their cultures, beliefs, family history and the geographic locations of their countries.

### China

Red eggs

Noodles

日本人通常在喜庆场合吃红豆饭，红豆饭也象征着吉祥。

### Japan

Red bean rice

### USA

Cake

### Egypt

埃及人在生日吃水果，水果象征着生命和成长。

Fruits

### France

Tarts

### India

印度人在生日等喜庆场合常常吃这种甜品。

Fried sweet balls

### Australia

Fairy bread

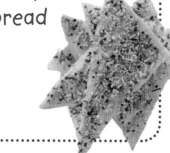

延伸活动：
问问学生自己国家过生日有什么习俗。

**1** Colour the birthday eggs red and the characters blue.

生 日 快 乐

**2** Can you locate the countries on the map? Write the letters.

a China   b Japan   c USA   d Egypt   e France   f India   g Australia

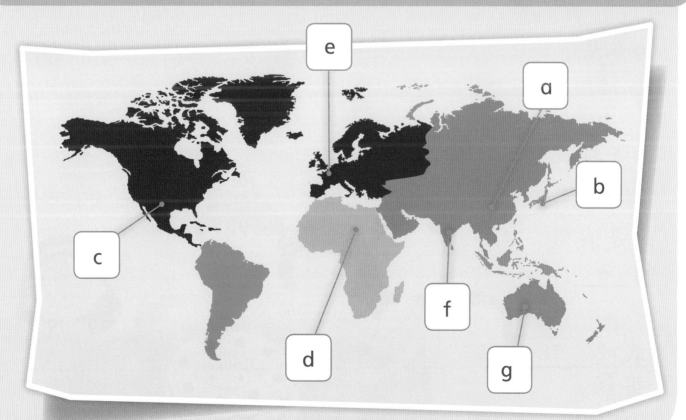

学生先几人一组，共同讨论，试将题目完成。随后，老师向全班展示一张标有各国家、地区的世界地图，和学生一起核对答案。最后看看哪一组的学生答对率最高。

## Checkpoint

**1** Write the letters to complete the conversation. Trace along the paths to find out whose pieces of cake they are. Then write the numbers.

提醒学生，每一个话框都只对应一个人物。在做连线题时，先确定某块蛋糕是与哪一个人物配对，再在蛋糕上方的圆圈内填入与人物对应的话框的号码。

a 蛋糕

b 怎么

c 做

d 快乐

e 一块

f 今天

g 生日

( 1 )  ( 7 )  ( 4 )  ( 2 )  ( 3 )  ( 5 )  ( 6 )

5 ___b___ 做
蛋糕呢？

4 这是我做
的 __a__ 。

6 我吃__e__
蛋糕。

评核方法：

学生两人一组，互相考察评价表内单词和句子的听说读写。交际沟通部分由老师朗读要求，学生再互相对话。如果达到了某项技能要求，则用色笔将星星或小辣椒涂色。

## 2 Work with your friend. Colour the stars and the chillies.

| Words and sentences | 说 | 读 | 写 |
|---|---|---|---|
| 今天 | ☆ | ☆ | 🌶 |
| 明天 | ☆ | ☆ | 🌶 |
| 昨天 | ☆ | ☆ | 🌶 |
| 怎么 | ☆ | ☆ | 🌶 |
| 生日 | ☆ | ☆ | 🌶 |
| 快乐 | ☆ | ☆ | 🌶 |
| 蛋糕 | ☆ | ☆ | 🌶 |
| 祝 | ☆ | 🌶 | 🌶 |
| 做 | ☆ | 🌶 | 🌶 |
| 块 | ☆ | 🌶 | 🌶 |
| 怎么庆祝呢？ | ☆ | 🌶 | 🌶 |
| 祝你生日快乐！ | ☆ | ☆ | 🌶 |

| Ask about how to do something | ☆ |
|---|---|
| Express good wishes to someone | ☆ |

1 今天是我的 ___g___ 。

2 祝你生日 ___d___ 。

3 这是谁 ___c___ 的蛋糕？

7 昨天你六岁，___f___ 你七岁，明天你八岁吗？

评核建议：

根据学生课堂表现，分别给予"太棒了！(Excellent!)"、"不错！(Good!)"或"继续努力！(Work harder!)"的评价，再让学生圈出右侧对应的表情，以记录自己的学习情况。

## 3 What does your teacher say?

# 分享 Sharing

延伸活动：
1 学生用手遮盖英文，读中文单词，并思考单词意思；
2 学生用手遮盖中文单词，看着英文说出对应的中文单词；
3 学生四人一组，尽量运用中文单词分角色复述故事。

## Words I remember

| 今天 | jīn tiān | today |
| 明天 | míng tiān | tomorrow |
| 昨天 | zuó tiān | yesterday |
| 怎么 | zěn me | how |
| 生日 | shēng rì | birthday |
| 快乐 | kuài lè | happy |
| 蛋糕 | dàn gāo | cake |
| 祝 | zhù | to wish |
| 做 | zuò | to make |
| 块 | kuài | piece |

# Other words

| 睡 | shuì | to sleep |
| 庆祝 | qìng zhù | to celebrate |
| 玩具 | wán jù | toy |
| 文具 | wén jù | stationary |
| 礼物 | lǐ wù | gift |
| 大家 | dà jiā | everyone |
| 忘记 | wàng jì | to forget |

# OXFORD
## UNIVERSITY PRESS

Oxford University Press is a department of the University of Oxford.
It furthers the University's objective of excellence in research, scholarship,
and education by publishing worldwide. Oxford is a registered trade mark of
Oxford University Press in the UK and in certain other countries

Published in Hong Kong by
Oxford University Press (China) Limited
39th Floor, One Kowloon, 1 Wang Yuen Street, Kowloon Bay,
Hong Kong

Illustrated by Anne Lee and Wildman

Photographs for reproduction permitted by Dreamstime.com

China National Publications Import & Export (Group) Corporation is an authorized distributor of
Oxford Elementary Chinese.

Please contact content@cnpiec.com.cn or 86-10-65856782

ISBN: 978-0-19-942984-4

10 9 8 7 6 5 4 3 2


Teacher's Edition
ISBN: 978-0-19-082206-4

10 9 8 7 6 5 4 3 2